# Kei Ca

## from Japan

1990 Honda Acty, photo by Mark Narus

# By Don Narus

## with Mark Narus

JKC122222

**Kei  pronounced "Kay"**
*Means light automobile in Japanese*

# Kei Cars
## From Japan

## By Don Narus
### with Mark Narus

Published and printed on premium white, type set in Arial, in the United States of America by LuLu Press, Inc., Durham, NC 27709. No part of this book may be duplicated or transferred in any format without the written consent of the author, with the exception of written reviews. Quotes and text excerpts are allowed where reference or credit is given to the work or the author.

Published, Printed and Distributed by
LuLu Press, Inc., Durham, NC 27709

First Edition

# Acknowledgments and Photo credits

The images in this book are digital, direct downloaded digital jpg images of various sizes. Some are original black and white (usually factory or archived photos). Others are original color converted to black and white using a grayscale process. While all images are necessary to the content of this book, their quality varies. The best images available at the time of publication, for the examples shown,were chosen. Every attempt was made to provide the best image available. We also realize that photos are subjective, when viewed through the lens of the viewer. If better images or a better conversion process becomes available after the initial publication they will be used in later editions. Copyright infringement of any photo is unintentional; and will be corrected when brought to our attention. We make every attempt to give credit to each photo where used in the book and on this page. If we missed someone, I apologize. It was not intentional. All photo and image sources are noted, where retrieved / downloaded from. Our thanks to the following:mitsuico.com, Royal-trading.jp, carsfromjapan.com, classiccars.com, japaneseclassics.com, nipponimports.com, sodo-moto.com, royal Trading.com, oldconceptcars.co, Bing.com, silodrone.com, El Cara Columbino, Carsandbids.com, google.com, M.narus collection, jspecauto.com, bringa trailer.com, JDM.com, toprankimports.com, carsfromjapan.com,JapanCar.com, Ebay.com, New England Motors, nwminitrucks.com, japancars.com, pinterest.com, beforeward.com, Japan Car FI, LLC,


Inside cover; Photo from Mark Narus

Front cover: Art Work by author

www.LuLu.com

# CONTENTS

## Chapter                            Page

www.lulu.com

アソビもシゴトもケイジドウシャと楽しむ夏。

# MAGAZINE
［Kマガジン］

August・2021
ccc
CAR LIFE LAB
Vol. **10**

わくわく海アソビ、どきどき山アソビ

# ケイと夏休み。

初サーフィン、サップ教室、親子バイクに絶景ピアノ etc.

DAIHATSU

冷蔵車します！

みんなのケイジドウシャ
**マニュアル車LOVERS**

かっこかわいく働いてます。
**MYワーキングバン**

# FORWARD

The Kei (K) car was first introduced in 1949, for the domestic Japanese market. Specification for the car were mandated by the Japanese government as to; wheels base, overall length, height, width and size of engine. The Kei, which means small, was aimed at the mass market, as a peoples car (ala VW Beetle). Kei cars were never imported into the USA. For that mater they were originally not for export, but in later years you did find them in England (UK), some European and third world countries. They began to show up more in the U.S. as collector cars and novelties. In order to to be legally imported into the U.S. The Kei car has to be at least 25 years old. That sounds like any model imported would need a lot of extensive restoration. NOT SO. Strict government controls on maintenance and a speed limit at 50mph. A lot of these cars are low mileage, well maintained, rust free, driveable examples. They may be 25 or more years old but they don't look it.

In order to get some idea as to size, I'm standing next to my son's 1990 Honda Acty van. I am 5ft-11in, tall and I could easily wash the roof without the aid of a stool. The van seats 5, it has its original paint, no rust, one crease in the side panel. It's equipped with a water cooled 3 cyl, 660cc, A/C, AWD, 5-speed manual.

Photo by Mark Narus

In 1949 the engine size was 150 cc, raised to 360 cc in 1951, the maximum length was 9.2 ft, raised to 9.8 ft in 1951, the overall height has remained at 6.6 ft through 2018. In 1955 the engine size was changed to 550 cc. The length changed to 10.5 ft and the width to 4.6 ft. In 1976 the engine size was increased to 660 cc and length to 10.8 ft. In 1998 length increased to 11.2 ft and width to 4.9 ft., engine size and height remained unchanged. The transmissions available were 5 speed manual and automatic.

Our book covers the so called 660 cc era, cars manufactured after 1990. some will have automatic transmissions or 5 speed manual, some with A/C, 3-point seat belts, rear defoggers, radial tires, AWD or FWD , some are turbo charged. By the way all Kei cars are right hand drive. We will be looking at the "K" sports cars, Vans and Trucks from familiar manufacturers as: Honda, Mazda, Suzuki, Subaru and Daihatsu. All major Japanese auto makers have built "K" cars, except Isuzu. These tiny cars from Japan are fun to drive, attract attention and are....well cute.

*Don Narus*

Image from Google.com

# Part 1: Kei Sports Cars

## Autozam AZ-1 by Mazda

Autozam is a Mazda brand name, in 1989 Mazda built a prototype Kei spec sports car, with an out sourced 550cc engine from Suzuki. The design was by Mazda's own design team led by Toshihiko Hirai, who also designed the Mazda MX-5. The prototype was introduced at the 1989 Tokyo Auto Show as the AZ-550.

Early renderings of the proposed AZ-550 prototype
Photos from jspecauto.com

A favorable response at the auto show put the 550-AZ into production as the AZ-1 in 1992. It was powered by a Suzuki sourced 657 cc turbocharged engine with two body colors available; Classic Red and Siberia Blue with the lower panels painted Venetion Gray, with a price tag of $12,400. Midway through the model year Mazda introduced the Mazdaspeed version; featuring an enhanced hood, a front spoiler and rear wing and a host of options, driving the price even higher. Timing is everything in the auto world and unfortunately, when the AZ-1 went on sale Japan had entered into a recession. Mazda found itself with the highest priced Kei sports car. The AZ-1 did not sell well having missed it's 800 units per month projection. Only 4,392 were sold that first year.

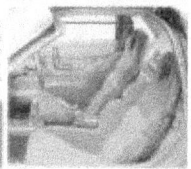

Image from oldconceptcars.com

# Mazda Autozam AZ-1 1992-1994

The Mazda AZ-1 is based on a redesigned Suzuki RS/3 concept, going though a series of redesigns which took over three years. It was finally released in 1992. Priced at $12,400 USD, making it the highest priced of its competitors. And if that wasn't enough, Japan was in the midst of a recession and only 4,392 were sold in its first year. Far below its projected sales of 800 units per month. In an effort to boost sales Mazda included an enhanced audio system as part of the standard equipment.

Photos from silodrome.com

The AZ-1 was available in only two colors; Siberia Blue and Classic Red, with lower panels painted in Venetian Gray. The gull wing doors are balanced and assisted by two struts. Opening and closing is effortless and entry into the vehicle is easier.

Photos from silodrome.com

Dashboard layout is straight forward with analog gauges and controls are in front of the driver, 3-spoke steering wheel with center horn push is attached to a tilt column. Standard features include A/C, center console, ergonomic bucket seats upholstered in gray cloth, and 3-point seat belts.

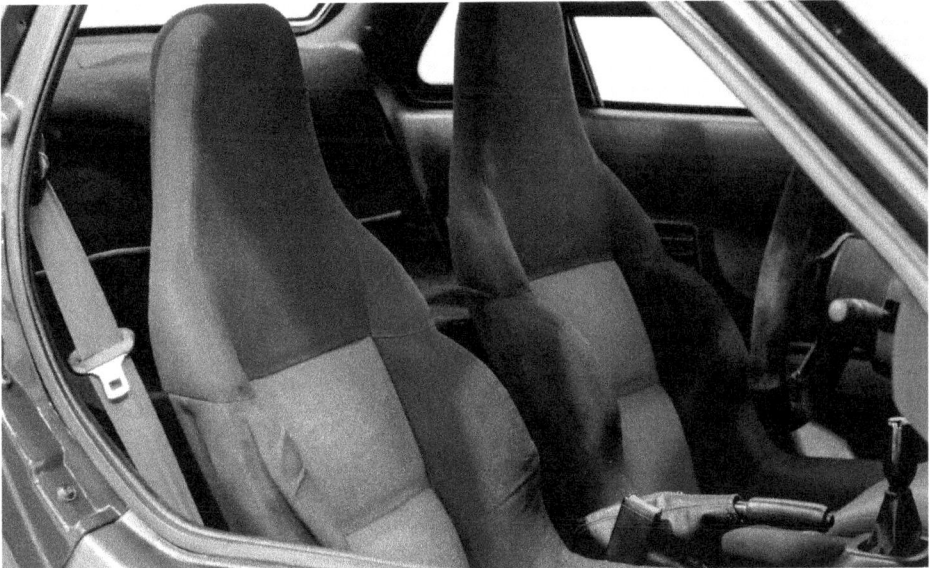

Photos from silodrome.com and El Caro Columbino

# Mazdaspeed AZ-1

In another attempt to gain a foothold in the Kei Market, Mazda came out with a special edition called, Mazdaspeed. A variation of the AZ-1 as a showcase for accessories available. The cars were available in solid colors and featured front spoiler and rear wing as standard with a host of options, ie; front and rear shocks with sport springs, LSD air filter, stainless steel and ceramic muffler, and alloy wheels.

Photos from carsandbirds.com

Interior features include; deep dish sport steering wheel, center console 5-speed floor shifter, solid color fabric covered ergonomic bucket seats.

Photos from carsandbirds.com

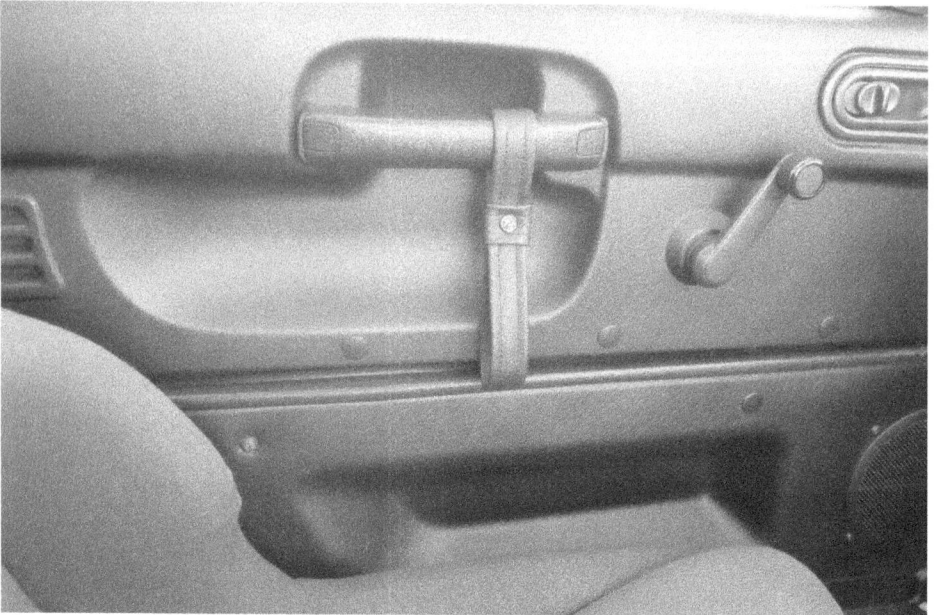

Note: The assist strap attached to door pull to help in closing the gull wing doors. The spare wheel and tire were covered and stored behind the seats. No power windows, or power seats.

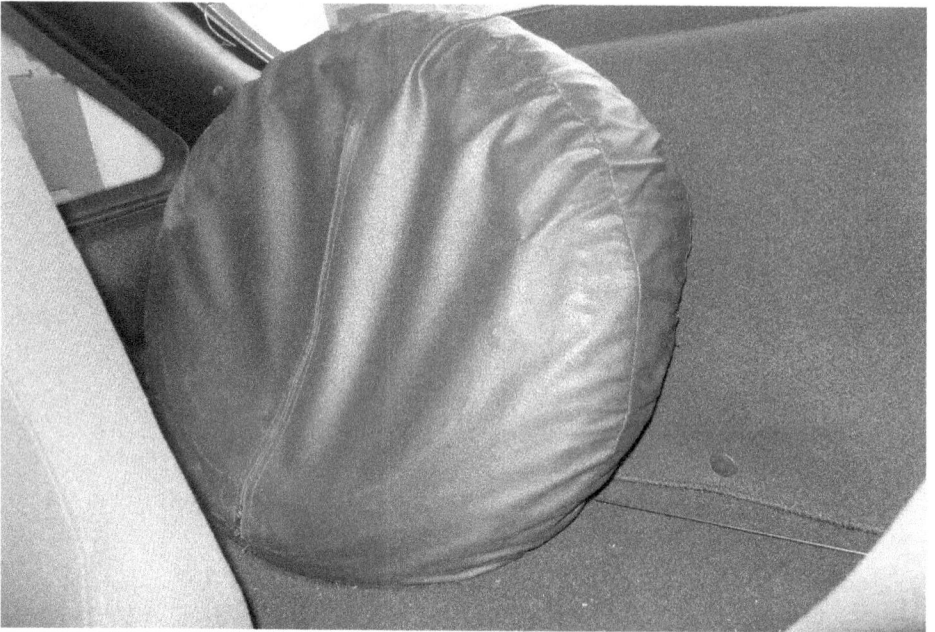

Photos from carsandbirds.com

Note: The headlight buckets were fixed with openings in the hood that fit around them when closed, The hood scoop fed air into the cabin. The wheel jack was stored under the hood, up against the firewall.

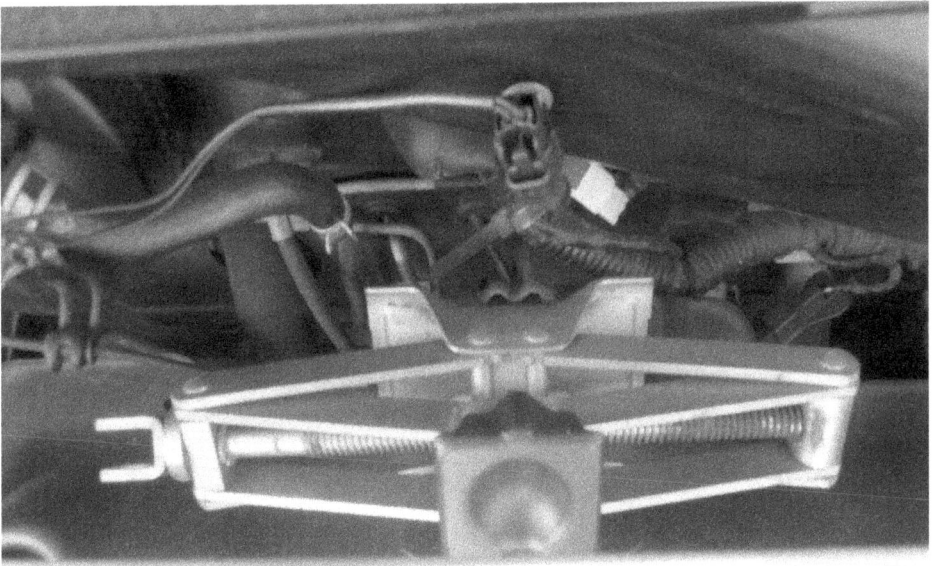

Photos from carsandbirds.com

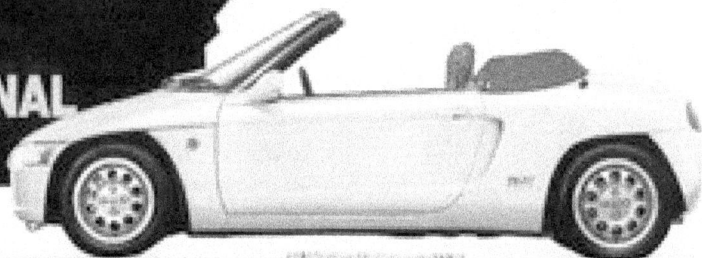

# 理屈ヌキに楽しく快適な

## 高密度 PERSONAL OPEN

# HONDA

# ふたりの「ビート」新登場!!

ホンダ「ビート」 Eアコンディショナー付
全国希望小売価格

**138.8** 万円

2人乗りのキュートなオープンボディに、
本格的ミッドシップ・レイアウトを採用。
空と光と、風と一体になるビートならでは
の快適なオープンエア・クルージング。
その快感を贈る人すべてに!!

◇高感度アイテム
「ビート・コレクション」も展開します。

# The Beat from Honda: 1991-1996

The Beat, designed by Italian design studio Pininfarina, was introduced by Honda in 1991. It was designed according to Japanese Kei specs. The Beat like other Kei cars was built for the domestic market only, not originally exported to the USA.

The Beat is a two seat roadster, powered by a transverse, 3-cyl, 656 cc (40 cu in), mid-engine, coupled to a 5-speed manual transmission.  It does not use a turbocharger or supercharger, instead it uses multi throttle response engine control ( MTREC) with throttle bodies for each cylinder to produce 63hp. The speed is electronically  limited to 84mph.

Sergio Pininfarina, CEO of  Carraozzeria Pininfarina,S.P.A.  And some early Beat renderings. The process; drawing, clay model, production.

Historically the Beat was the last car approved for production by Soichiro Honda, CEO and founder of Honda Motors. He died in 1991 at age 85.

# 1991 Honda Beat 1991-1996

The x-ray tells the whole story; mid engine, coil spring suspension, the wheels set at the far corners, with little overhang front and rear, excellent stability. The Beat had the longest wheelbase of all the Kei cars. It was available in two models; the PP1-100 and PP1-110. Outwardly they looked pretty much the same, with some cosmetic up-dates. However the PP1-110 model had a number of mechanical differences.

Photos from google.com and carsandbids.com

The standard Beat features: air conditioning, power windows, 3-point seat belts, sun visors, front stabilizer, halogen headlights, soft canvas top, steel wheels, laminated glass windshield, and tempered door glass. Color choices; Red and yellow. Special versions; "F" Aztec Green Pearl, and alloy wheels. "C" Captiva Blue Pearl, or Blade Silver Metallic, and white alloy wheels, "Z" Everglade Green Metalic, plus three black gauges, mud guards rear spoiler, alloy wheels and exhaust pipe tip.

Photos from bringatrailer.com

Taillight lenses included back-up light. Headlights were encased halogen,

The door handles were flush. The air intake helped with engine cooling.

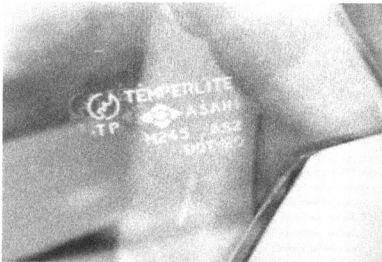
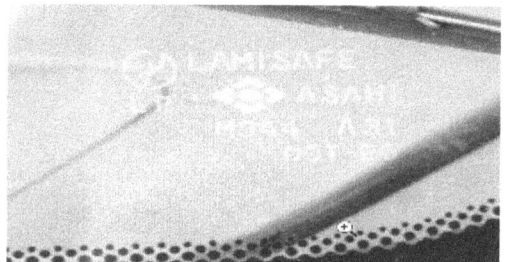

**Above left**, door glass is tempered. **Above right**, windshield is laminated.

<u>Note;</u> the short front and rear overhangs do to wheel placement.

Photos from bringatrailer.com

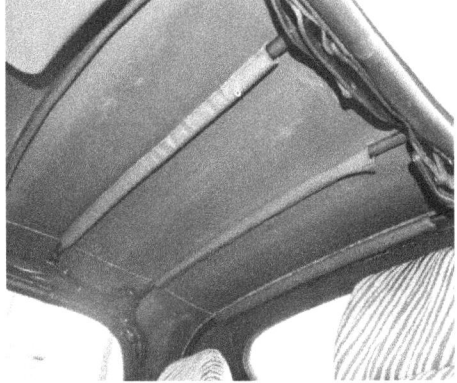

The canvas top was manually operated. It had five bows enabling it to be folded and tucked into a small space, it was also easily removable.

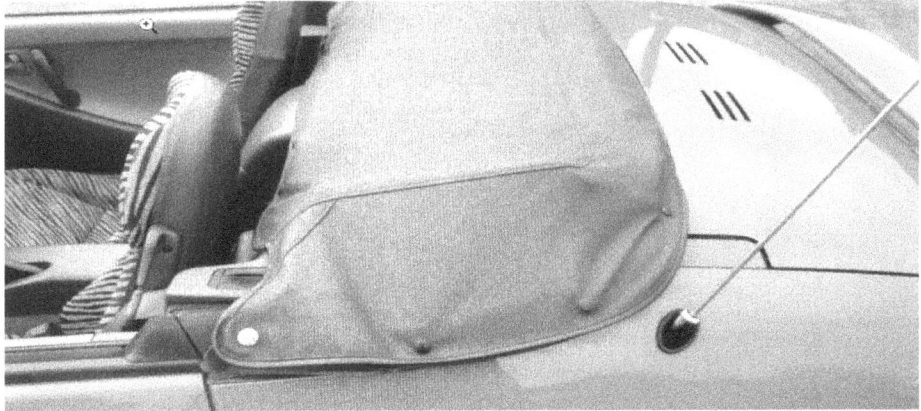

Photos from bringatrailer.com

Up front under the hood is where the spare was stored and all the fluids were checked. In the mid section behind seats sat the engine, a 656cc, 63 hp, 3 cylinder water cool engine with individual throttle bodies, called MTREC (Multi Throttle Responsive Engine Control) capable of 84 mph.

With the canvas top removed access to the engine is gained easily by unfastening a panel. Any room left over at the rear is considered storage.

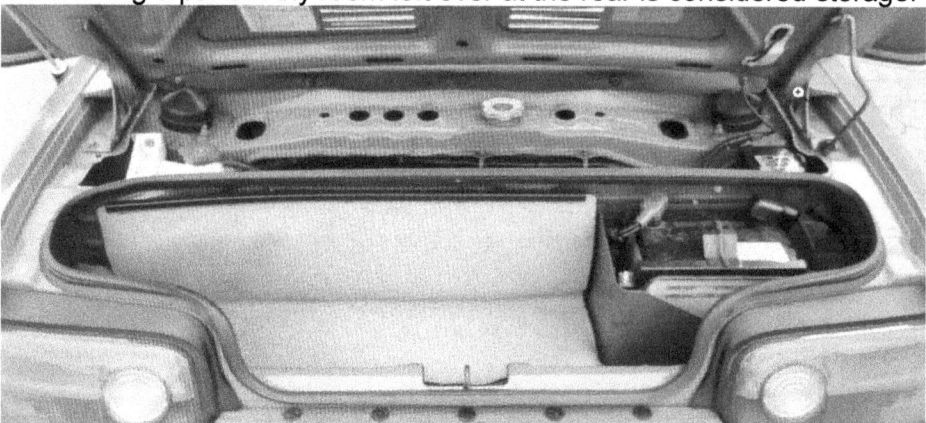

Photos from bringatrailer.com

24

Cloth upholstery in a zebra stripe pattern with matching floor mats, ergonomic bucket seats, 3-point seat belts, A/C, full console all standard.

Photos from bringatrailer.com

Key start ignition switch and console compartment with aux speaker.

The center console housed the power window switches and an ash try. No cup holders, however; remove the ash try and wha-la' a cup holder

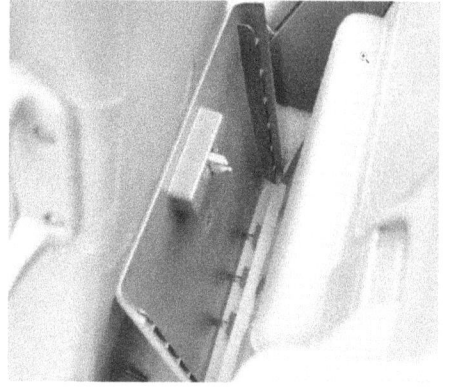

Need a place to hide your stuff? How about this compartment behind the drivers seat back. Big enough for important documents. It's lockable.

Photos from bingatrailer.com

Image from google.com

Image from Ebay.com

28

# The Cappuccino from Suzuki 1992-1998

Suzuki began working on a Kei car in 1987 and in 1989 it introduced the Cappuccino, a 2-place sports car. Keeping to the mandated specs for a Kei car, the new entry had a wheelbase of 81.1 inches an overall length of 129.7 (10ft-8in) width 54.9 in and a curb weight of 1,598 lbs. The wheelbase was 9 in shorter than the Honda Beat and 77 lbs lighter. It was closer in size and weight to it's other competitor the Mazda AZ-1. But its design was far more unique than either of it's competitors.

The engine was placed mid-front with a rear wheel drive. The weight distribution claimed to be 50/50. It combined the features of the AZ-1 (Hardtop coupe)and the Beat (convertible top). It was classified as a roadster without a soft top. The aluminum roof panels could be removed making it a Targa T-top. The roll bar and rear window could be folded, making it a convertible or you could leave all in place and have a hardtop coupe. The roof panels are stored in the trunk and the roll bar and rear window retract into a space behind the seats.

Suzuki originally designed the Cappuccino for its homeland market only. Production started in 1991, as a 1992 model, which was release to the public in November of 1991. From November 1991 through the 1992 model year 15,113 units were produced. Soon after its introduction Suzuki of England approached the Corporation about selling the car in the UK. After much discussion the Cappuccino under went 23 changes to conform to the British NTA. From 1993-1995 1,110 cars were sold in the UK from a allocation of 1,182 cars. The balance of 7 cars were sold in Germany, France, Netherlands and Sweden. After which no more cars were shipped out of Japan. The Suzuki management decided UK sales did not justify the changes that had to be made to comply.

Unlike it's competitors the Cappuccino could be a coupe, a Targa T-Top (by removing the roof panels) or a convertible (by stowing the roll bar and rear window). Also unlike the competition the rear window has curved glass. The overall design was based on the wedge, low front, high rear.

Photos from bing.com and JapanCar.com

When removed, the roof panels are stored in the trunk. The "B" pillar roll bar and glass rear window are manually folded into a well, behind the seats. <u>Note</u>:The massive hings used for the rear window and roll bar.

Photos from JDM.com and toprankimports.com

Standard; all vinyl ergonomic bucket seats, 3-point seat belts and adjustable head rests. <u>Note:</u> gas cap release lever in center console.

Photos from  carsfromjapan.com

Photos from japancars.com

HVAC controls, AM/FM stereo radio, digital clock, lighter, make up console panel up front. **Opposite page:** Steering wheel with air bag, wiper and light controls, 3-speed automatic shifter, power window controls, rear window defogger and remote side mirror controls. **Shown below,** back of center console (between the seats) with a courtesy light.

Photos from japancars.com

The trunk looked adequate, but you stored the roof panels there wasn't much room,for anything else. The spare was stored under the trunk mat.

The 657cc,63hp, turbocharged 3-cylinder engine was pushed against and into the firewall giving it a mid-front location. Access was straight forward, pretty much as you find in any conventional engine compartment.

Photos from japancar.com

Image from pinterest.com

# Part 2: Kie Vans

## The Acty Van from Honda

The Kei Van evolved from the Kei Truck. The same mandated specs that cover the truck also apply to the van. The first Kei Vans based on the Kei truck platform and cab forward design appeared in the 1960's with the introduction of the Suzuki CARRY in 1964.

Over the succeeding decades the Kei van has been refined to where it now meets a new modern set of Kei specs. Our book will deal with what's known as the 660cc generation of Kei vans. The generation of vans from the 1990's.

The Honda Acty Street van second generation started in 1988. The Acty truck version has round headlights, while the van has large squares. It's the only Kei van to have a mid-engine rear wheel layout, with access panels in the cargo floor. Standard equipment in our 1990 example van includes: tinted windows, rear window defogger, a/c, AM/FM stereo, disc front brakes and drum rear, AWD, 3-point seat belts, 4-way emergency flasher, laminated glass windshield and tempered glass door, quarter panel and rear windows.

In 1990 the engine was changed from 547 cc to 656 cc. The new power plant generated 63hp and could do 65 mph, ( in 1996 fuel injection was added which boosted hp to 71) coupled to a 5-speed manual or 3-speed automatic. It has a wheelbase of 74.8 in, overall length of 129.7 in, width of 54.9 in, and height of 68.9 in.

The 1990 Acty Street van is based on the Acty truck platform with the cab over design, which means that everything behind the front seats is cargo area for the truck, while in the van this area has additional seating plus cargo area. Vans appeal to families, young buyers as well commercial use as taxis, resort shuttles and delivery conveyances.

Photos from M.Narus collection and Ebay.com

All instrument gauges ware centered in a cluster pod in front of the driver. Controls for HVAC and radio are situated to the left, within easy reach. Comfortable bucket seats, adjustable head rests, durable woven cloth upholstery, floor mounted shifter, wall-to-wall carpet front and back with floor mats, 3-point seat belts are all standard.

Photos from m.narus collection

Left side of the dashboard features storage trays atop dash, generous glove box with additional storage under dash. No usable area was overlooked. The front seat headrests were both adjustable and removable and differed in style to the rear headrests.

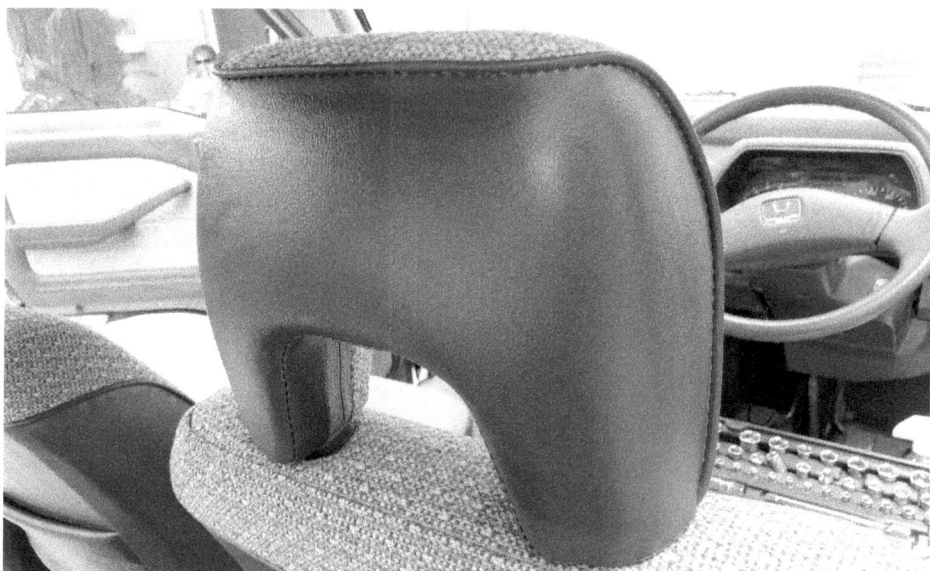

Photos from m.narus collection

There are two individual rear seats upholstered in sturdy woven cloth with adjustable and removable headrests, (Note: style difference in the rear headrest) and a folding arm rest that separates the two. With the arm rest folded there is room for another passenger. The complete seat assembly can be folded and stored in the floor well. **See next page.**

Photos from m.narus collection

Rear seats fold easily for storage in foot well. The seats are stored level with the cargo floor and increases that space considerably.

Photos from m.narus collection

The entire rear of the van lifts as a hatch, providing easy access and a roof overhang for tail gating. With the floor carpet mat removed, and with various panel covers removed, provides ample access to the engine.

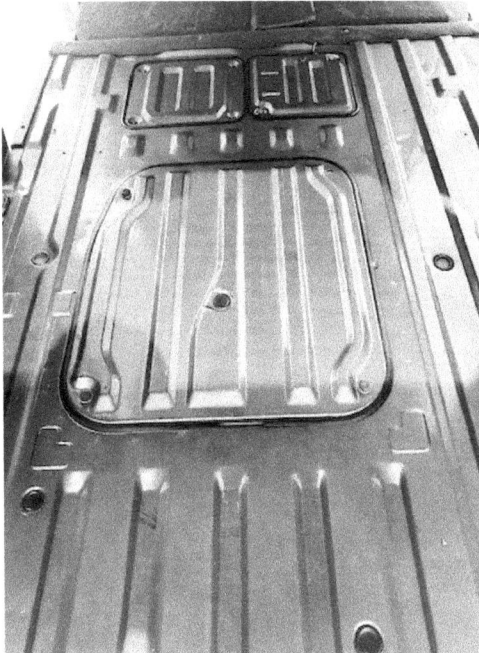
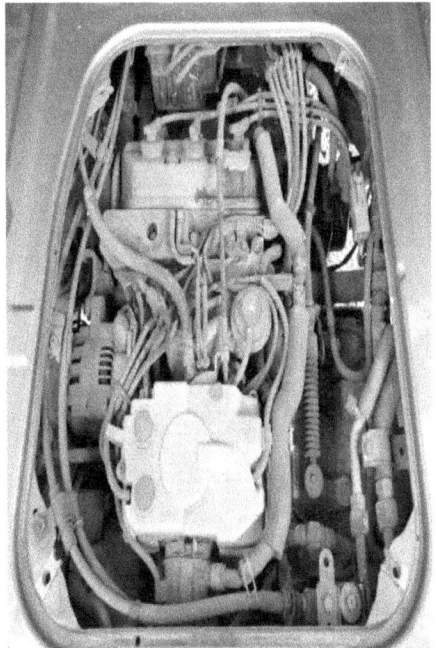

Photos from m.naurs collection and bringatrailer.com

# The Carry Van from Suzuki

The Suzuki Carry Van, based on the Carry Truck was first introduced in 1961. It had gone through Eleven Generations of upgrades and design changes. We are covering the Ninth Generation, 1991-1999 and our primary example is a 1992 model.

Suzuki Carry van was changed to the Suzuki Every van in 1982. It is powered by a 657cc engine, mounted mid-way, with a rear wheel drive, coupled to a 5-speed manual or 3-speed automatic.

In 1993 and 1995 it received some up-grades, front drum brakes were changed to disc, the wheel bolt pattern was changed from 4x114.3mm to 4x100mm, and the turn signal lights were changed to amber.

Photo from New England Motor Cars

Large windows all around provide excellent 360 visibility. Wheel covers are painted white. **Below,** the conventional dash is similar to the Acty.

Photos from New England Motor Cars and nwminitrucks.com

The front seat backs re-cline, upholstery is cloth, the head rests are adjustable and removable, 3-point seat belts are standard. The rear seat is a bench type with room for three passengers and it folds flush into the foot well providing additional cargo room.

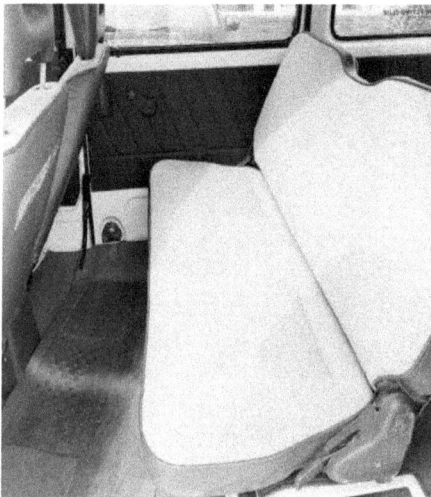

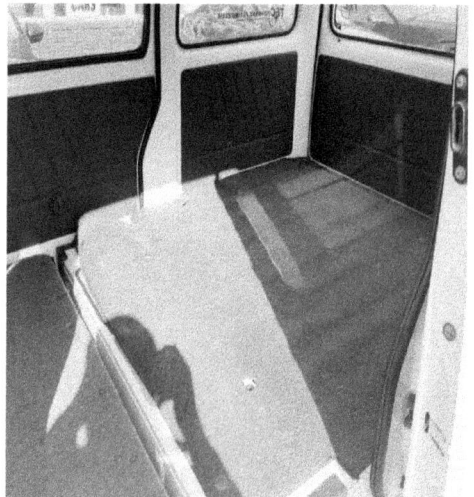

Photos from New England Motor Cars

# The Bravo Van from Mitsubishi

Mitsubishi first introduced their "K" van in 1968 with the Minicab design. In 1989 the Brovo van was added as an upscale model van.

The Bravo had a front engine four wheel rear drive layout and was equipped with a 657 cc engine,coupled to a five speed manual transmission. It had an overall length of 128.5 inches. One inch loner than the truck it was based on.

Features included an automatic free wheel hub and the first manufacturer to offer a sliding sun roof, three speed automatic transmission, rear window wiper, power brakes, squared headlights, larger bumpers and two tone paint .

The upgraded Mitsubishi Bravo. AWD, 657cc engine, automatic trans.
Photo from carsandbids.com

Note: Rear spoiler, panoramic roof windows, sun roof, power windows and door locks. A/C, radio with cassette player and three point seat belts.

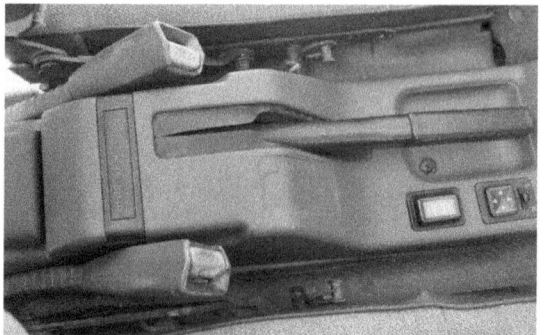

Photos from crasandbids.com

Seats are upholster in heavy duty wear resistant cloth. Head rests are adjustable and removable. Rear seats are split, with folding arm rests. There is ample leg room. Sliding doors open from either side.

Photos from carandbids.com

Rear seats fold flush into the foot well. The front seats have a unique feature by pushing the seat backs forward you can reverse the seating; instructions for this feature are stenciled on the side of the seat cushion. Pretty slick.

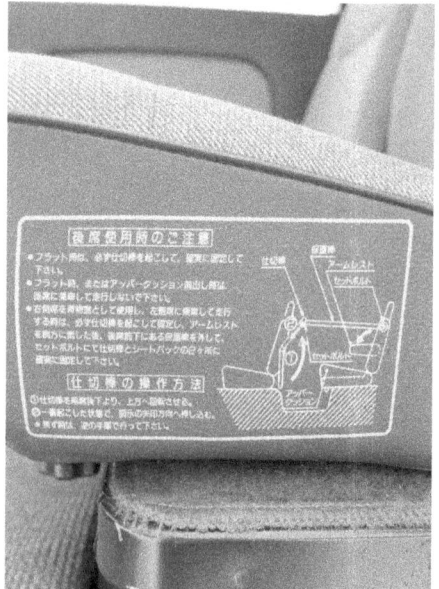

Photos from carsandbids.com

# The Hijet Van from Daihatsu

Daihatsu is owned by Toyota, so while Toyota under its own name does not produce a Kei vehicle, its subsidiary does and has since 1960.

The Daihatsu Hijet van is a cabover design with a mid-front (over the front wheels), rear wheel-drive or AWD. It's powered by a 660cc water cooled DOHC turbo charged engine since 1994, coupled to a 5-speed manual or 3-speed automatic.

The 1994 Hijet was the beginning of the eight generation, which lasted till 1999. It was first shown at the "30th Tokyo Motor Show in October of 1993. As part of the eight generation a special edition was available, the "Double Deck" AWD. In May of 1999 an EV version was introduced as the Hijet EV.

In 1980 the two millionth Hijet was produced,and in November of 2020 sales in Japan reach an estimated 7.4 million.

The 1994 Daihatsu Hijet van powered by a 660cc water cooled engine available in either two wheel or four wheel drive, automatic or 5-speed.
Photo from carsandbids.com

The Hijet features extra large rear quarter and rear hatch windows. The rear window wiper is standard, wheel covers are painted. Dashboard layout is conventional. Rear bench-seat folds flush into the foot well.

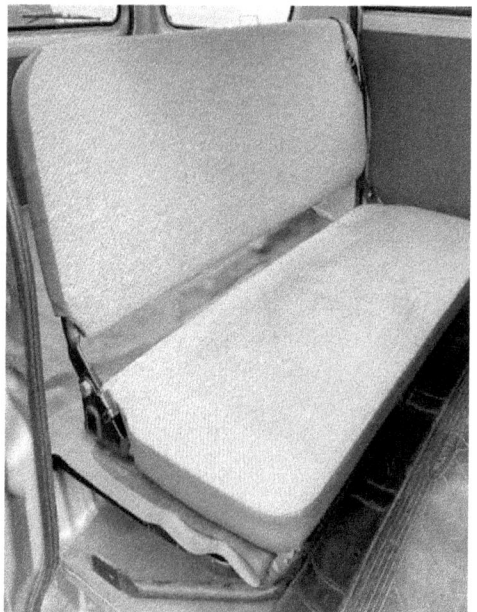

Photos from carsandbids.co

This special Hijet version called the "Double Deck was first introduced in 1986, it is considered a 4-door van. In the U.S.A. It would be an extended cab pick-up. It has a 660cc engine, 5-speed manual and AWD.

Photos from Japan Car FL, LLC

# The Sambar Van from Subaru

The Subaru Sambar van was first introduced in 1961. It had a rear engine rear drive configuration and a body on frame rather than a unibody construction. Its styling cues came from the Volkswagen type 2 Samba van of 1951-1967.

It was the first Kei truck to use the cabover set-up, also it was the last Kei compliant vehicle to use the rear engine, rear wheel drive.

In 1990 the fifth generation was introduced with an upgraded 660cc engine. Options included a 3-speed automatic transmission. Special edition packages were also offered, including a retro version called the "Dias Classic".

The 1995 Subaru Sambar with 660 cc engine, AWD and 5-speed manual.
Photo from mitsuicoLtd.com

Large windows all around are a feature. Conventional dash layout with HVAC controls to the left. <u>Note</u>: The column mounted tachometer.

Photos from mitsuicoLTD.com

Rear seats feature a folding arm rest and two cup holders with a center console. The seats fold down flat  and are stored in the foot well . The head rests are removable and can be stored in rear side pocket.

Photos from mitsuicoLTD.com

The 1995 Suburu retro special edition "Dias Classic", it had all the specs and mechanical fearues of the Sambar. The interior was identical to the Sambar. The center grille and two side grilles were non-functional.

Photos from Japan Car Fl. LLC

# The Scrum Van from Mazda

The Mazda Scrum van was first introduced in 1989 as a cabover microvan, sold only in Japan. The name came from a rugby maneuver that implies toughness.

The Srum complies with all the government mandated Kei specification, including length, width, and height; it is in fact a re-badged Suzuki Carry/Every van, using the Suzuki 660cc engine and drive train.

It is avaiable in 2WD or 4WD. The 4WD can be switched betwwen 4WD and 2WD. Standard features include, A/C, radio, disc brakes, 5-speed manual or 3-speed automatic.

The 1996 Mazda Scrum, is a re-badged ninth generation Suzuki Carry/Every. The Scrum was first introduced in 1989, sold only in Japan.
Photo from royal -trading.jp

Standard four bolt pattern steel wheels, sliding side door both sides. The dashboard has conventional layout. Right hand drive, 5-speed manual with part time AWD. The HVAC and radio controls on left.

Photos from royal-trading,jp

Seats are upholstered in a blue hue basket weave pattern cloth. Head rests are vinyl covered, adjustable and removable. 3-point seat belts are standard. The rear seat is a bench, high back, no head rests. It folds up against the the front seat back rests. Cargo area has a carpet mat,

Photos from royal-trading.jp

# The Clipper Van from Nissan

In 2003 Nissan entered into an agreement with Mitsubishi to rebadge its Minicab as the Nissan Clipper van. It was powered by a water cooled, 660cc, three cylinder 48hp,power plant coupled to a 5-speed manual transmission. With a front engine, rear wheel drive layout. The 3-speed automatic transmission was optional.

Other optional equipment included; air conditioning, power steering, power windows and driver side air bag. There were no modifications to the exterior or interior.

The 2003 Nissan Clipper van was a rebadged Mitsubishi Minicab. The agreement lasted till 2012, when Nissan switched to a rebadged Suzuki.
Photo from  carfromjapan.com

The dash features two cup holds and dash mounted 3-speed automatic shifter and HVAC controls. Air bag in steering wheel. Power windows and power door lock switches were mounted in door panels.

Photos from  carfromjapan.com

Headrests are built into the seat backs. Rear bench seat folds and is stored in foot well. Access to engine under front seat cushions.

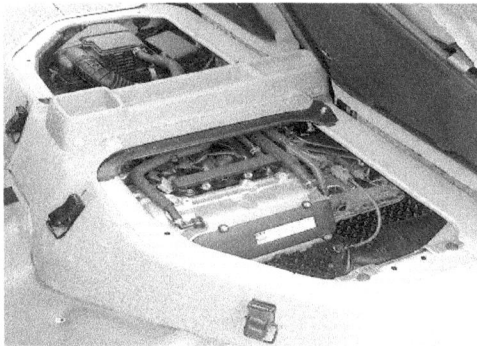

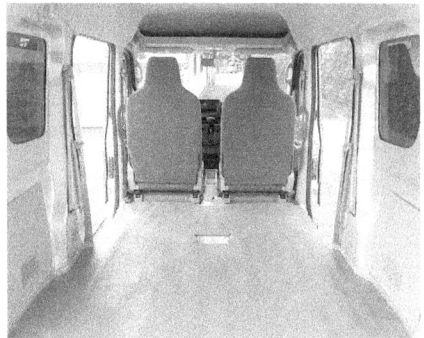

Photos from carfromjapan.com

頼りになる奴！
ミニキャブ5

50年規制合格・新規格車
500ccで新登場!!

Image from google

# Part 3: Kei Trucks

The Kei truck first appeared shortly after the end of World War II. The Japanese government realized the need for affordable transportation in both the private and commercial sectors.. They came up with mandated specs that would fill the need and challenged their vast auto industry to raise to the task. Taking design cues from the Volkswagen Type 2, (which filled a similar need in Germany) auto makers developed the Kei Truck (which means small or micro)

In its day the VW type-2 was consider a micro or mini vehicle, with a 8ft wheelbase, 14ft overall length, 5ft width and 6ft height.12 inches shorter than the Beetle with the same wheelbase and width as the Beetle. I am sure the government officials in Japan took this into consideration when planning the Kei specifications

Photos from wikipedia.com

The first cabover Kei truck appeared in 1959, it was called the Kuogane Baby, built by the Kurogane Company from 1959 to 1961. It looked a lot like the VW Types-2 truck, available in two configurations; pick-up and van.

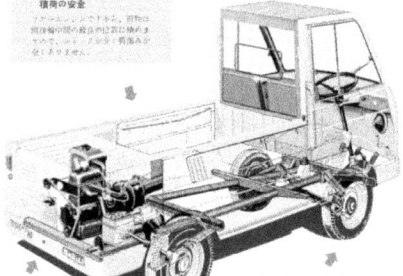

The Kurogane pick-up above and the van below. 1959-1961.
Photos from wikipedia.com

# The Acty Truck from Honda

The Honda Acty (short for Activity) was first introduced in 1977. It was designed to be an economical work truck, with no frills, no luxury option, but it did offer air conditioning, power steering and some trim. It had a mid engine, rear wheel drive layout.

Mandated specifications for the Acty were the same for all manufacturers. Maximum length 134 inches, width 58 inches,and height 79 inches. Engine size was mandated but placement was up to the individual manufacturer. The Acty had a mid engine with a rear wheel drive layout.

Over the years the the mandated specs were upgraded. The Acty went through four generations covering over four decades. The model we will cover is the second generation 1988-1999 with the 660cc engine.

The 1990 Acty micro pick-up truck, the second generation Kei.
Photo from  classiccars.com

The cargo bed was roughly 4ft x 6ft, however both side panels and the tail gate folded down, providing a much larger area for a wider load.

Photos from classiccars.com

The Acty featured split seats, 3-point seat belts, adjustable and removable head rests not part of the seat back but mounted on separate brackets. Extra storage under the hinged seat cushion. This particular example is equipped with A/C, AWD, 5-speed manual and AM radio.

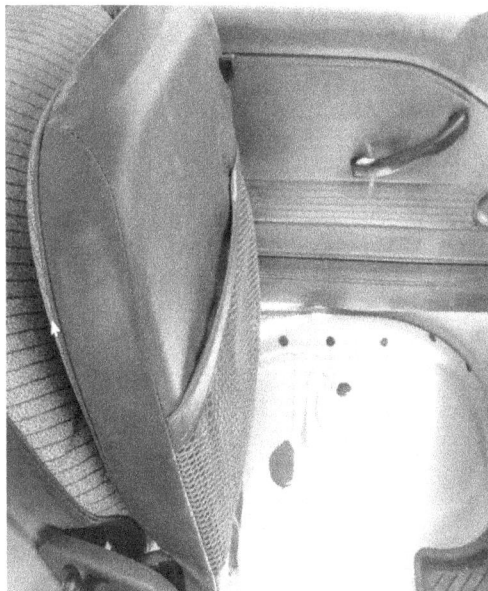

Photos from classiccars.com

# The Sambar from Subaru

The Subaru Sambar (a name similar to the VW Type-2 Samba) was the first that complied with the governments mandated commercial Kei specs. First introduced in 1961 the Sambar went through eight generations.

We are covering the fifth generation 1990-1999, the 660cc era.  The Samba has a rear engine, rear wheel drive configuration. The standard engine is carburetted with  three cylinders.  A supercharger with fuel injection is optional. A 5-speed manual is standard with an optional automatic. Four wheel drive was also available. AWD standard.

The Subaru Sambar in its fifth generation. The cabover design is typical of the Kei truck, a design common to all micro trucks
.
Photo from carsandbids.com

Standard 6ft bed with folding sides and tailgate. A unique option was the "Dump Bed". Hinged at the rear with a center hydraulic arm that lifts the bed to a 60 degree angle. Handy option for landscapers.

Photos from carsandbids.com and bing.com

Speedometer and gauge cluster in front of driver, HVAC controls and radio in a console to the left. Storage trays atop dash, split vinyl seats.

Photos from carsandbids.com

# The Carry from Suzuki

The Suzuki Carry truck was first introduced in 1961 in the cabover design. By 1991 it had entered into its ninth generation, which was commonly known as the 660cc era referring to the size of the engine. Kei specification had evolved during this period with the most significant changes in size of engine.

As to styling, most of the changes were cosmetic, usually confined to headlight shape and placement and bumper size. The Carry had a mid-engine, rear wheel drive configuration. The engine itself was three cylinder, water cooled, developing 63hp and coupled to a 5-speed manual transmission with an optional 3-speed automatic.

Its overall size conforming to mandated specs was approximately, 10ft in length, over 4ft in width and 6ft in height with a 6ft wheelbase.

The ninth generation Suzuki Carry received a mild facelift in 1995
Photo from japaneseclassics.com

The cabover design was used by all manufacturers in building the Kei trunk and every bit of usable space was utilized.

Photos from japaneseclassics.com

The dash featured a cluster in front of the driver that housed all gauges, speedometer, HVAC controls and radio. Between split seats the shifter, emergency brake and if equipped with 4WD, the axle lock lever. 3-point seat belts were standard, headrests adjustable and removable.

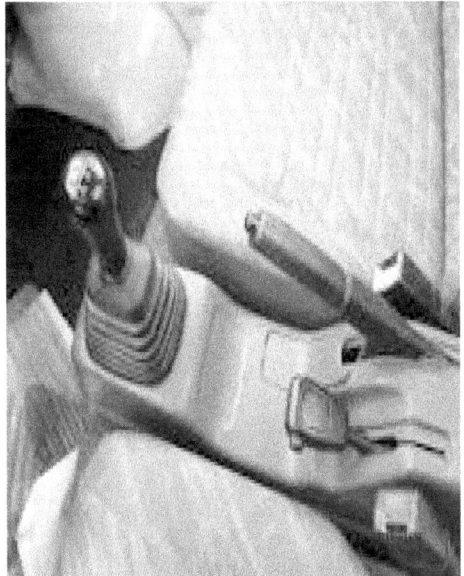

Photos from japaneseclassics.com

# The Hijet from Daihatsu

The Hijet Kei truck manufactured by Daihatsu was first introduced in 1960. The name implies "midget". In 1994 it began its eight generation, with some changes in power plants. It was now powered by a water cool,3 cylinder, 660cc, rated at 63hp, capable 75 mph. During 1980 the two millionth Hijet was produced.

Daihatsu continued to us the front mid-engine, rear wheel drive or AWD or 4WD configuration. The new power plant was coupled to a standard 5-speed manual or optional 3-speed automatic.

In 1997 Turbo power was available, along with anti-lock brakes. Turbo charged still maintained 63 hp as mandated for a Kei truck.

Photos from nipponimports.com

The cabover design for the Kei truck was the same for all manufacturers.
A  4ft x 6ft bed with sides and tailgate that folds down.

Photos from nipponimports.com

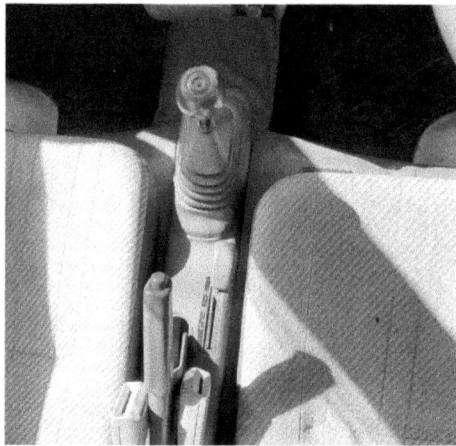

The dashboard layout was conventional with everything in front of and within easy reach of the driver. Split seats with the shifter, emergency brake, and axle lock (for 4WD) between them.

Photos from nipponimports.com

# The Minicab from Mitsubishi

The Minicab debuted in 1966 and complied with the mandated specs laid out by the Japanese govern for Kei (small) trucks. It had a front engine, rear wheel drive layout or a front engine 4WD.

Initially it was powered by a 359cc two stroke, two cylinder, air cooled engine. In 1987 the two cylinder was replaced with a three cylinder 546cc engine. A supercharger was also added. In 1990 the 546cc was replaced with a 660cc. A free wheel hub had replace the axle lock, on all 4WD models.

The 1990 model also received a minor face lift adding larger front and rear bumpers. With the larger bumpers the overall length was increased to 127 inches, still within the mandated specs.

Mitsubishi Minicab first introduced in 1966 was upgraded with a 660cc, 3 cylinder engine in 1990. Like its competition it is a cabover design.
Photos from nipponmotors.com

The dashboard has a conventional layout but with a unique angular design. Very stealth looking. Note: The 4WD axle lock next to the emergency brake. Split seats, standard 3-point seat belts, adjustable and removable headrests. Floor mounted 5-speed manual shifter.

Photos from sodo-moto.com

# The Scrum from Mazda

The Scrum Kei truck sold by Mazda is a cabover rebadged Suzuki Carry. Introduced in 1989. It is powered by a 660cc, 3-cylinder, water cooled DG/DH51 Suzuki engine, with a mid-engine, rear wheel drive layout.

The Scrum was available in either 2WD or 4WD. It can also be switched between 4WD and 2WD with high and low ranges.

The name Scrum, was borrowed from the game of Rugby, and is a maneuver indicating toughness.

The Scrum as a rebadged Suzuki Carry, follows the same cabover design as all other Kei trucks. With a water cooled 660cc, 3-cylinder, mid-engine, rear wheel layout. It has a 5-speed manual transmission and disc brakes.
Photo from commons.wikipedia.com

The dashboard layout is the same as the Suzuki Carry, except for the embossed steering wheel Mazda logo. Familiar cabin set-up.

Photo from royaltrading.com

# The Clipper from Nissan

Nissan entered the Kei domestic Japanese market in 1966 when it merged with Prince Motor Company and began selling a rebadged version of the "Prince Clipper".

In 2003 Nissan began selling a rebadged version of the Mitsubishi Minicab. Then in 2013 when Mitsubishi announce it would no longer build the Minicab, Nissan switched to Suzuki and began selling a rebadged version of the Carry.

The Prince Clipper as it appeared in 1958, with the weird front sheet metal. Nissan began selling a rebadged version in 1966 when it merged

with the Prince Motor Company. The truck referred to as Nissan Clipper. In 2003 Nissan switched to a rebadged Mitsubishi Minicab and continued to call it the Nissan Clipper. In 2013 they switched to Suzuki.

Photos from beforward.com and carfromjapan.con

Note: passenger seat is larger, access to engine compartment is under passenger side seat cushion. Headrests, adjustable and removable, are attached to seat backs, unlike other Kei trucks.

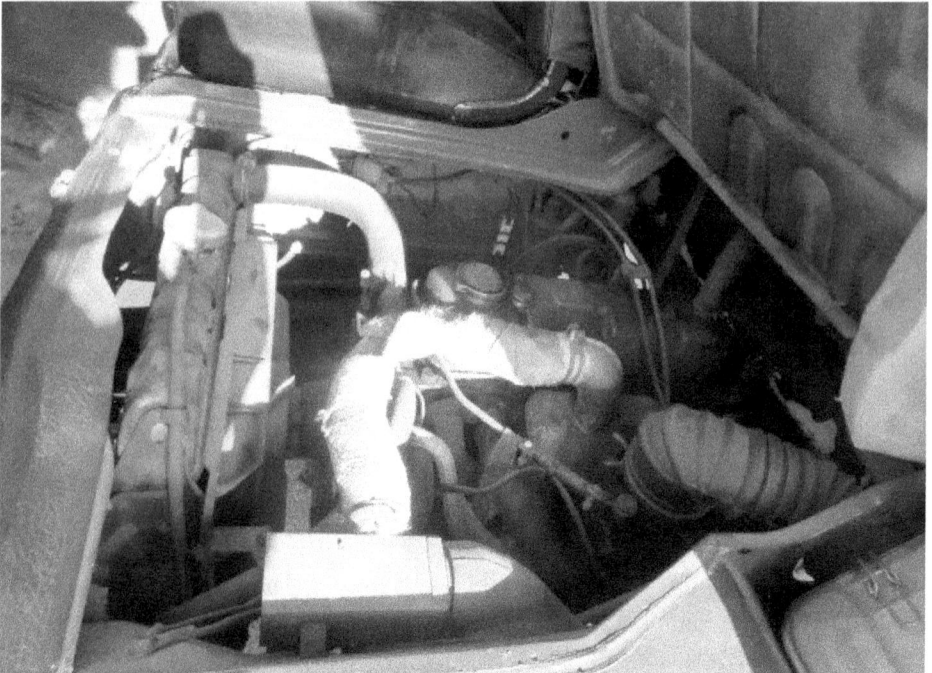

Photos from carfromjapan.com

Shown here is the 1978 Prince version of the Nissan Clipper truck.

Photos from beforward.com

Photo image from bingimage.com

# Resource and References

Nissan Clipper
www.wikiwand.com

Daihatsu HiJet
wwww.wikipedia.com

The Little Kei Fire Truck
integrityexports.com

Kei Cars-Everything You Need to Know
By Ken Nakashima
jdmexport.com/blog/best-Kei cars

Kei Vans
www.wikipedia.com

Kurigane Baby
www.wikipedia.com

Kie Trucks are Weird, an legal in U.S.
Autotrader.com

Kei Cars: They're Tiny, Japanese
and Awesome
Carsforsale.com

Kei cars, trucks, and vans
Japan Car, Florida, LLC
Oldsmar, Fl.

So You Think You Want a Japanese
Domestic Market Import
By Sam Bayer
Published 2021  Class Winner

Mitsubishi Minicab
www.wikipedia.com

Mazda Scrum
Autozam Scrum
www.wikipedia.com

Mini-Truck State Laws
www.iihs.org/ laws/
minitrucks.aspx

Kei Truck
www.wikipedia.com

Kei Cars
www.wikipedia.com

Minicars:Cheap,Cheerful
Peter Nunn
www,jama-english.html

Honda Beat Kei car
Hemmings Motor News

Kei Sports Car
The Throttle

Catching on in the U.S.
Danyell Mashal
Motor Biscuit

Japanese Mini Truck
By Mark Roehrig
Trafford Publications 2020

プリンス
クリッパー

# About The Authors......

Authors Don Narus with son Mark Narus, taking delivery1990 Acty Van.

<u>Don Narus</u>  is a nationally  recognized auto historian who has chronicled the automobile for over five decades and has written over 60 books on the subject. His writing style can be characterized as conversational; like talking to a friend. His books are both entertaining and informative. They make great primers and handy reference guides.

<u>Mark Narus</u>  is a Industrial Engineer, with an MBA in business, and is employed by a Florida regional financial institution. He is a auto enthusiast; in addition to the Acty van, he owns 2 BMW Motorcycles, a Vespa Scooter, and an Electric bicycle,. He has owned a 1969 Beetle Convertible, a 1965 Mustang Convertible and a Chrysler Woodie "K" car, a  Chrysler "K" convertible and a 1985 Ford Ranger.

# Other Titles......

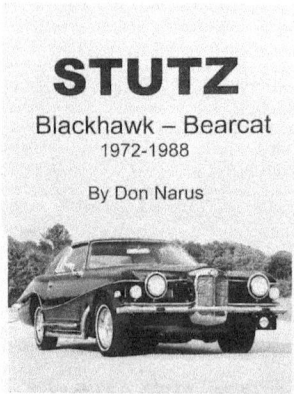

**STUTZ**
Blackhawk – Bearcat
1972-1988

By Don Narus

American
**PLAYBOY**

Don Narus

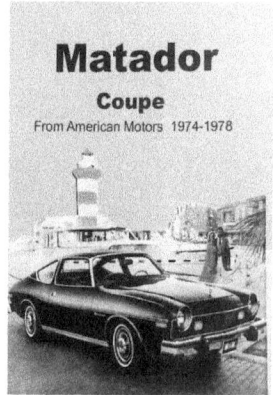

**Matador**
Coupe
From American Motors 1974-1978

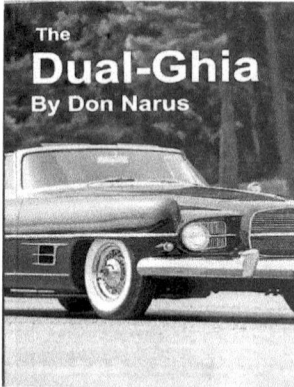

The
**Dual-Ghia**
By Don Narus

**Rambler
American**
1964-1969

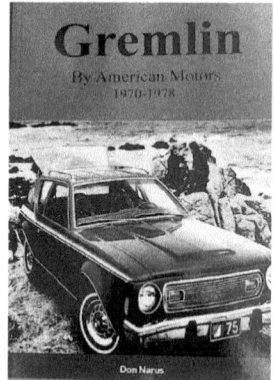

**Gremlin**
By American Motors
1970-1978

Don Narus

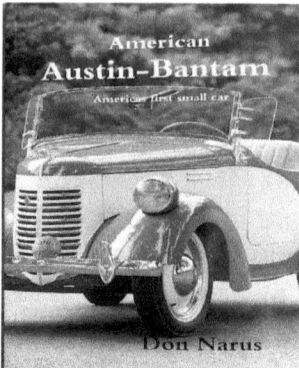

American
**Austin-Bantam**
America's first small car

Don Narus

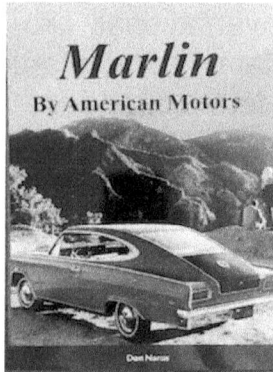

*Marlin*
By American Motors

Don Narus

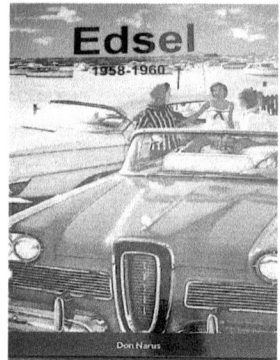

**Edsel**
1958-1960

Don Narus

These and many more titles by Don Narus are available from on-line book sellers such as Amazon.com, Barnes and Noble.com, Old Milford Press.com or direct from the publisher www. LuLu.com.

Milton Keynes UK
Ingram Content Group UK Ltd.
UKHW021002160924
448404UK00013B/726

9 781387 499489